12 STORIES ABOUT HELPING ANIMALS

by Patricia Hutchison

12 STORY LIBRARY
MORE TO EXPLORE

www.12StoryLibrary.com

12-Story Library is an imprint of Bookstaves.

Photographs ©: hedgehog94/Shutterstock.com, cover, 1; American Society for the Prevention of Cruelty to Animals/PD, 4; PD, 4; santypan/Shutterstock.com, 5; eike/CC2.0, 6; Kleber Cordeiro/Shutterstock.com, 7; IrinaK/Shutterstock.com, 8; US Government/PD, 8; Enrique Aguirre/Shutterstock.com, 9; Kids Saving the Rainforest/YouTube, 10; PD, 11; LMortell/Shutterstock.com, 11; Cineberg/Shutterstock.com, 12; Connie Fitzgerald/Shutterstock.com, 12; Elena Rostunova/Shutterstock.com, 13; boyphare/Shutterstock.com, 14; Dave Matthews Band/YouTube, 14; Craft0logy/CC2.0, 15; Roop_Dey/Shutterstock.com, 16; wanphen chawarung/Shutterstock.com, 17; Joseph C/Shutterstock.com, 17; World Wide Fund for Nature/PD, 18; Steve Tum/Shutterstock.com, 18; Barcroft TV/YouTube, 19; Snap2Art/Shutterstock.com, 19; denisgo/Shutterstock.com, 20; Ruptly/YouTube, 20; Vitalinka/Shutterstock.com, 21; Thomas Ponce/YouTube, 22; Jiri Prochazka/Shutterstock.com, 23; CatwalkPhotos/Shutterstock.com, 23; World Animal Protection/PD, 24; Jess Kraft/Shutterstock.com, 24; Just dance/Shutterstock.com, 24; World Animal Protection Africa/YouTube, 25; The Intelligencer/YouTube, 26; resusapet.com, 27; Rich Carey/Shutterstock.com, 28; Dmytro Zinkevych/Shutterstock.com, 29

ISBN
9781632357410 (hardcover)
9781632358509 (paperback)
9781645820260 (ebook)

Library of Congress Control Number: 2019938686

Printed in the United States of America
October 2019

About the Cover

A veterinarian cares for a horse.

Access free, up-to-date content on this topic plus a full digital version of this book. Scan the QR code on page 31 or use your school's login at 12StoryLibrary.com.

Table of Contents

1 ASPCA: North America's Oldest Humane Society

Henry Bergh founded the ASPCA in 1866.

In 1863, an American diplomat named Henry Bergh was on assignment in Russia. One day, he came upon a carriage driver. The man was beating his fallen horse. Bergh stopped the beating and saved the horse. He believed that animals should be treated with kindness and respect. Wanting to make a difference, Henry returned to America. On April 10, 1866, he founded the American Society for the Prevention of Cruelty to Animals.

Nine days later, New York State passed the first animal protection law in the United States. The law allowed the ASPCA to investigate complaints of cruelty to animals. The organization was also allowed to make arrests. Henry Bergh worked hard for animals. He inspected slaughterhouses. He worked with police to close down dogfighting pits. He gave lectures on animal rights.

Today the ASPCA works to help animals in three areas. First is the rescue of animals that are being harmed. But help doesn't

end there. After the rescue, they find the animal a safe home. ASPCA's second job is to provide health services. The society runs a veterinary hospital and an animal poison control center. Outreach is the third important area. The ASPCA provides training and donations to animal groups throughout the United States.

$13 million

Money the ASPCA gave to animal shelters and organizations in the Gulf Coast region in 2005

- The area was hit hard by Hurricanes Katrina and Rita.
- The ASPCA sent staff to help rescue animals.
- It also donated money to shelters that allowed people with pets.

FROM ANIMAL RIGHTS TO HUMAN RIGHTS

Bergh's animal rescues were a model for people who wanted to protect children. In 1874, a child in New York was found beaten and tied to her bed. This prompted some people to take action. They founded the New York Society for the Prevention of Cruelty to Children.

2

Endangered Species Act: A Law Protecting Animals

Under the ESA, species can be listed as endangered or threatened. Endangered means the species is in danger of becoming extinct. Threatened means the species is likely to become endangered in the near future. Almost any plant or animal species can be added to the endangered species list. Only insect pests cannot. The ESA protects listed animals from human actions that would destroy their habitats.

Healthy plants and animals are needed for a healthy environment. When a species is lost, it triggers the loss of other plants and animals. Human lives depend on healthy ecosystems. In 1972, US President Richard Nixon called on Congress to do more for conservation. He wanted a new law that would protect species from extinction. On December 28, 1973, the Endangered Species Act (ESA) was signed.

487

Number of nesting pairs of bald eagles in 1967

- The bald eagle was put on the endangered species list that year.
- By 2007, there were 4,215 nesting pairs.
- The US Fish and Wildlife Service removed eagles from the list.

These include logging, drilling, and other activities.

The ESA has saved many animals from extinction. Numbers of bald eagles and gray wolves have increased. Populations of marine animals such as sea turtles and whales have also risen.

But not everyone has accepted the ESA. Some think it gets in the way of economic development. When an endangered animal is found in a particular area, the use of that land or water is strictly regulated. This affects farming and logging. Some people have asked for more research on the economic effects of the law.

Sea turtle populations have increased as a result of the ESA.

3

Manatees: Gentle Giants Making a Comeback

Manatees are the elephants of the sea. In 1967, the gentle mammals were placed on the endangered species list. They often collided with speedboats. Their water was being polluted. Their habitat was shrinking. In 1991, aerial surveys counted only 1,200 manatees swimming in the waters of Florida. The US Fish and Wildlife Service took action.

The Service, together with other agencies, created more than 50 manatee protection areas. The US Coast Guard took charge of watching over the sanctuaries. They ticketed speeders. There were fewer

Manatee populations continue to recover because of the efforts of the US Fish and Wildlife Service.

collisions between manatees and boats. Fishing was restricted. Fewer manatees became tangled in fishing gear. Manatee organizations rescued dozens of manatees each year. Most were released back into the wild.

In January 2017, spotters saw more than 6,000 manatees in the Florida waters. This was the third year in a row they saw so many. As a result, the Service reclassified manatees from endangered to threatened.

The Service is still committed to helping the manatees recover. The marine mammals will be protected, even though they have been reclassified. Conservation efforts made a huge difference for manatees. By 2018, the estimated population in Florida was over 7,000.

14
Length in feet (4.3 m) of a manatee

- Manatees can weigh over 3,000 pounds (1,360.8 kg).
- They are grayish-brown in color.
- They have fine hairs on their bodies and bristles around their mouths.

MISTAKEN IDENTITY

Manatees are large marine mammals. They have two flippers in front and a large, spoon-shaped tail. Stories are told about sailors thinking manatees were beautiful mermaids. Scientists nicknamed them sea cows because they eat ocean grasses.

4

Kids Saving the Rainforest: Helping in Costa Rica

Janine Licare in 2015.

Janine Licare grew up near the rainforest in Costa Rica. She knows the rainforest helps the earth in many ways. The trees give us oxygen to breath. Millions of species live there. Many haven't even been discovered yet. The rainforest might also contain the cures for many diseases. As a young girl, Licare watched as people destroyed it.

In 1999, when Licare was just nine years old, she set out to save the rainforest. She and her friend Aislin Livingstone painted rocks and bottles. They sold them at a roadside stand and made $80. They used the money to buy four acres (1.6 hectares) of forest land. But the girls never knew where the money went.

The two friends decided to start their own organization. They called it Kids Saving the Rainforest (KSTR). With a small loan, they bought five acres (2 hectares) in the middle of the rainforest. They sold pieces of the land for a dollar each to pay back the loan. Many years later, the loan was finally paid off.

Now an adult, Licare is the head of KSTR. The organization has grown since 1999. Today it works on

120

Number of animals KSTR rescued in 2010

- The organization has a wildlife rescue center with two veterinarians.
- They were able to release more than half of the rescued animals back into the wild.
- Some of the animals have come back to visit.

Licare's efforts have helped the endangered Titi monkeys in Costa Rica.

many projects. One of KSTR's main concerns is to save endangered Titi monkeys. Volunteers plant trees to give the monkeys food and shelter. They build bridges to help them cross the roads safely. Their hard work is paying off. In KSTR's first 10 years, the monkey population more than doubled. Janine also teaches workshops for children. She is trying to show younger generations how important it is to preserve the rainforest.

5 Gucci: A Famous Fashion Designer Goes Fur-Free

People have mixed feelings about fur fashions. To some, they are glamorous. To others, they represent cruelty to animals. In recent years, the clothing industry has become more fur-free. Gucci, the famous Italian fashion company, has joined in. It is partnering with the Fur Free Alliance, an international organization.

Since the spring of 2018, Gucci has not sold fur fashions. Under the new policy, it stopped using any animal raised or caught for its fur. The company went a step further. It sold all of its leftover fur fashions at a charity auction. Then it donated much of the money from the auction to the Humane Society of the United States. Gucci gave the rest to an animal protection organization in Italy.

Gucci's leaders realized that many fashion buyers do not want fur products. Consumers know that animals are brutally killed to make them. The company hopes its example will cause a ripple effect around the world. Maybe it will encourage other brands to stop using fur. Animal fur fashions will be a thing of the past.

Protesters during London Fashion Week.

40+

Number of animal protection organizations in the Fur Free Alliance

- Members of the alliance work together to end the killing of animals for their fur.
- They inform the public about the cruelty animals suffer from the fur industry.
- They encourage the fashion industry to use alternatives to fur.

HIGH-TECH FAUX FUR

Technology is now available to make luxurious fake fur. Many companies are using this instead of real fur. Unreal Fur is made in Australia. Its products look and feel like natural fur. FURious Fur fashions are made from microfiber yarns. Some look like real fur. Others are dyed bright colors. These clothes are sold around the world. They remove the need for animal cruelty.

6 Reteti Elephant Sanctuary: Warriors Saving Elephants

At the Reteti Elephant Sanctuary in Kenya, workers watch a plane land. They carefully remove the cargo. It is a two-year-old elephant that has lost his mother. The workers pour water on him to keep him cool. Then they move him to a stall. Veterinarians begin to examine him.

Every man who works at the Reteti is a Samburu warrior. The Samburu are a semi-nomadic tribe in East Africa. They raise cattle, goats, sheep, and camels. They live a traditional way of life. Not long ago, elephants were their enemies. But the Samburu have learned that elephants feed on low bushes and trample small trees. This helps the grasslands grow. There is more food for their animals. The humans and the elephants are learning to live together peacefully.

The Reteti takes in orphaned or abandoned elephant calves. The goal is to release them back into the wild herds that live nearby. Not all the elephants at the Reteti can be

Baby elephants are well cared for at the Reteti Elephant Sanctuary.

released right away. The older ones help watch over the younger ones. They teach them how to strip leaves for food and take mud baths.

Keepers are trained to take care of the elephants. Feeding is a big part of their work. They feed the calves special formula every three hours. Sanctuaries like the Reteti are needed because elephant numbers are dwindling. Elephants are being killed by ivory poachers.

2016

Year when the Reteti Elephant Sanctuary opened

- The Retiti is located within Kenya's second-largest elephant population.
- There are 6,000 elephants in this part of Kenya.
- In the Retiti's first year, nearly 30 young elephants were rescued.

HELPING THE ELEPHANTS HELPS THE COMMUNITY

All the keepers at the Reteti Elephant Sanctuary are from the local community. They are paid for their work. The Reteti is providing new opportunities to Samburu women and people who didn't go to school.

7

Tigers: An Endangered Species on the Rise

Throughout Asia, tigers face constant threats. Poachers kill them for fur. Deforestation is destroying their habitat. The wild tiger population has dropped over 95 percent over the last century. Tigers are an endangered species. In 2016, Cambodia declared its tiger population extinct.

However, tiger populations are on the rise in some countries. In 2010, representatives from 13 Asian governments attended a Global Tiger Summit in Russia. The countries promised to double the number of wild tigers by 2022. They called this the TX2 campaign. The countries that are most committed include Russia, India, Nepal, and Bhutan. They are seeing the most progress.

In parts of Asia, more than 5,000 tigers live on farms. They will be killed and made into rugs, wine, and medicines. Conservation organizations in these countries want to end the consumer demand for tiger products. They also want governments to adopt a zero-poaching policy.

Tigers are endangered, but their populations are increasing.

Early in the 20th century, more than 100,000 tigers roamed the world.

THINK ABOUT IT

Every part of the tiger from head to tail is traded in illegal markets. The tiger trade brings in millions of dollars every year. Knowing what you now know, would you ever buy a tiger rug?

In 2010, there were only 3,200. But TX2 efforts are helping. By 2016, the number had risen to almost 3,900. The decline of the tiger population has stopped. But tigers are still not safe. Governments and communities continue to take action to make sure their numbers increase.

121

Number of tigers in Nepal in 2009

- By 2013, the number had increased to 198.
- This is a 60 percent increase in 4 years.
- Nepal is on track to achieve its TX2 goal.

8

World Wildlife Fund: Bringing Back Rhinos

In 2018, the World Wildlife Fund released a report. The news was bad. More than 4,000 species declined between 1970 and 2014. That is 60 percent of the world's wildlife population. WWF has worked for more than five decades in over 100 countries. Their mission is to protect all life on earth. Their fieldwork has helped save several species from extinction. These include tigers, giant pandas, and rhinos.

Rhinos are one of the oldest groups of mammals. They once roamed across Africa and Asia. But today few survive in the wild. WWF is working to increase rhino populations. Its Black Rhino Range Expansion Project (BRREP) in South Africa creates new populations in different areas. The animals are removed from parks with large populations. They are taken to places where the numbers of rhinos have dropped drastically.

First, the rhinos are sedated. The workers put straps around the animals' ankles. The rhinos are lifted into the air by helicopter. They fly upside down for about 10 minutes

WWF

100,000

Number of rhinos in the early 1900s

- Today only about 5,000 exist.
- Many rhinos are killed by poachers.
- WWF works to help train law enforcement to stop poachers and save the rhinos.

until they reach an open space. Then they are lowered, loaded into crates, and driven to their destination. Once they arrive, the animals are released unharmed into their new home. Almost 200 rhinos have been relocated by BRREP. Over 80 new calves have been born. Since the project began in 2003, the rhino population has increased over 20 percent.

It's not painful for a rhino to have its horn removed. According to wildlife veterinarians, it's like having your fingernails filed.

THINK ABOUT IT

Rhinos are killed by poachers for their horns. Many people believe the horns are powerful medicine. The WWF has started to harmlessly dehorn rhinos. Do you think this is a good idea? Why or why not?

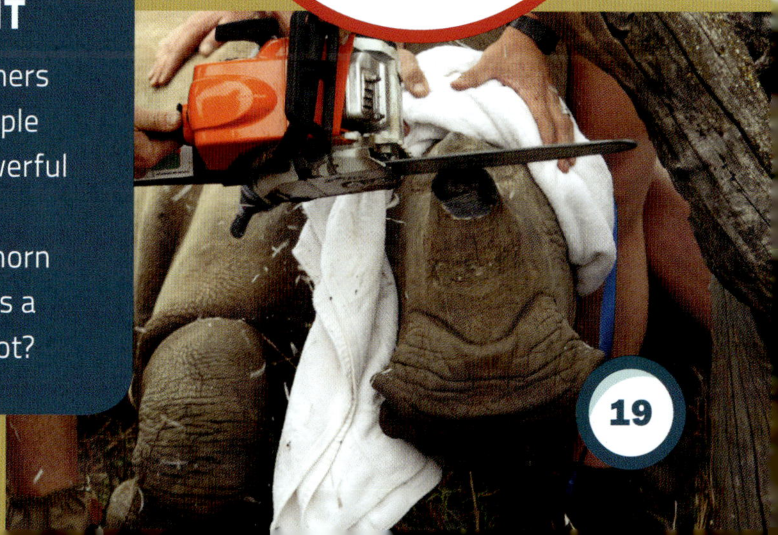

9

Turtle Tunnels: Saving Slow Movers from Fast Trains

Railroad tracks can be a danger to slow-moving turtles. In Kobe, Japan, turtles were finding this out the hard way. To get to a pond, they had to cross the tracks at a switch point. Many turtles were squashed between the blades of the switch. Some of them died. West Japan Railway officials worked with a turtle expert to find a way to help.

After conducting a few experiments, they came up with a solution. The

5

Number of tunnels built under the railroad tracks in Kobe

- The West Japan Railway had help from the Suma Aqualife Park to build the tunnels.
- The tunnels were completed in November 2015.
- Railway officials hope to keep using this system in the future.

Wildlife bridges are good for animals and vehicles.

SAFELY CROSS HERE

Animal bridges and culverts are being built over and under highways across the globe. The Netherlands is leading the way. It has more than 66 animal crossings. They protect badgers, boars, and deer. But these safety measures are not just for large mammals. A bridge in Australia helps millions of red crabs over a busy road. In Washington State, a special rope bridge guides squirrels across a highway.

railway installed shallow tunnels beneath the tracks. The U-shaped ditches are made of concrete. Now the turtles can walk under the tracks directly to the pond. The tunnels were built at two points along the track that were most dangerous for the turtles.

In less than a month, 10 turtles were saved. Rail workers inspect the tunnels regularly. They look for injured animals. Any that are found are brought to the Suma Aqualife Park nearby for care. Officials hope the tunnels will also be helpful to humans. When turtles fall into the switches, they cause train delays. The tunnels should prevent this from happening.

10

Thomas Ponce: A Teen Speaks Up for Sharks

Thomas Ponce knows that animals can't speak up for themselves. So he has stepped up to speak for them. Ponce has been an animal rights activist since he was four years old. One of his strongest passions is protecting sharks. He is teaching people about the horrors of shark finning. This is the practice of catching a shark and removing its fin. Then the shark is released to slowly die in the ocean.

Ponce's love for sharks began on a pier in Florida. He watched a man catch a baby bonnethead shark. The man was going to kill it and eat it. After 20 minutes of pleading, Ponce convinced the man to let him release the shark. Holding the shark in his hands, he felt an instant connection. He knew then he wanted to protect sharks forever.

Thomas Ponce in 2013

73 million

Estimated number of sharks killed every year

- Sharks are the ocean's top predators.
- Over 10,000 sharks are killed per hour.
- Some shark populations have been reduced by 90 percent.

Although shark finning is banned in US waters, it continues in many other countries where fishing is less regulated.

At the age of 12, Ponce founded a group called Lobbying for Animals. The group made a presentation to representatives from the US Congress. They proposed banning the sale of shark fin products. They also proposed laws to make sure sharks that are caught are not finned.

Today Ponce is the coordinator of a site called Fin Free Florida. He is trying to raise awareness of the dangers sharks face. He points out other issues the earth's oceans are facing. He also works with a group called Shark Angels. Together, they defend the sharks. They broadcast messages on the importance of keeping the oceans clean. Ponce knows that healthy oceans keep the earth in balance. By saving the oceans, humans are saving themselves.

11

World Animal Protection: Stopping Wildlife Selfies

Illegal loggers in Peru cut down a 100-foot (30.4-meter) tree. A sloth at the top holds on tight. The tree crashes to the ground. Somehow, the sloth survives. But it is quickly bagged up, taken to a market, and traded for a few dollars. Then it is sold into the tourist trade. The sloth is kept in a dirty, cramped cage. Tour guides use it to sell animal selfies to tourists.

The wildlife selfie craze is a worldwide sensation. Many tourists take part in it. Most love animals. They want to be near them. They don't know the animals are treated cruelly. Vila São Pedro in Brazil is a popular spot for selfie tourism. There, it also affects children. Tourists like to take pictures of the animals with local children. Many kids are leaving school to make money.

World Animal Protection is trying to help. The organization works with local schools. It helps children

THINK ABOUT IT

Tourists share their wildlife selfies on social media. This encourages others to do the same. It creates a cycle of cruelty for the animals. What would you say to a friend who is eager to take a selfie with captured wildlife?

250,000

Number of people who have signed World Animal Protection's Wildlife Selfie Code

- People can sign the code on the organization's website.
- The site educates users about the harmful treatment of animals used in selfies.
- Users commit to taking only cruelty-free selfies.

understand the need to support wildlife. Consultants and teachers use many different activities. They teach kids how to treat animals in a caring way. Students also learn about ecosystems and nature conservation.

DON'T take a wildlife selfie if:

- I'm being held, hugged or restrained
- You're baiting me with food
- I could harm you

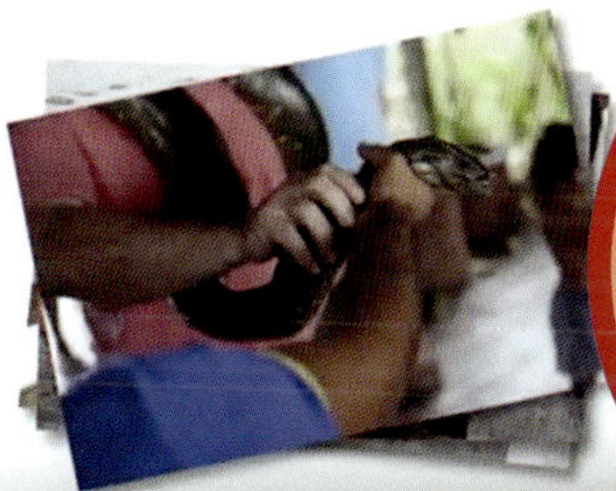

> People who sign the Selfie Code commit to taking only cruelty-free selfies.

Some of the children have become Wildlife Leaders. They give presentations to the community. They tell what they've learned about the cruelty of animal tourism. They ask adults to help protect animals. World Animal Protection is hoping more communities will get involved with the project.

12

Emily Rilling: Helping First Responders Rescue Pets

Most kids ask for heaps of presents for their birthday. Emily Rilling isn't one of them. For her 12th birthday, she wanted to do something to help animals. So she hosted a dog party and raised $888. She used the money to buy 13 pet oxygen mask kits. Then she donated them to her local fire department in Eddington, Pennsylvania.

Both pets and people can suffer from smoke inhalation during a fire. When this happens, they can't breathe. Pet oxygen masks are like the ones used to revive humans who aren't breathing. But they have a special design. They fit over the snouts of animals. Each one has a rubber edge. This seals the air

Emily Rilling demonstrates how the pet oxygen mask works.

170

Number of pet oxygen masks Emily Rilling has donated

- After Rilling donated the first 13 mask kits, other fire stations asked her how they could get some.
- People who heard about her project donated money
- Rilling gave the kits to almost 80 fire stations.

A BETTER IDEA FOR PETS

Before firefighters had the special masks, they used children's equipment on pets. It didn't work as well as the pet masks do. Eddington's fire chief thinks the masks are a great idea. The station thanked Emily for her hard work and donated $700 to her organization.

inside. Each kit contains a small, medium, and large mask. They can be used on dogs, cats, and smaller animals such as rabbits. Tubing connects the mask to the oxygen tank.

Rilling calls her project Emily's Resus-A-Pet Oxygen Recovery Mask Mission. Her idea has spread quickly. Her project receives many donations. With the money, her program has expanded to other counties. Emily knows that pets are like family. She feels good knowing her work is helping animals survive fires.

Ways You Can Help

- Reduce plastic use. Plastic waste can end up in the ocean. This is harmful to marine life. Sea turtles, sharks, whales, and birds can choke on plastic bags. Plastic straws are also harmful.
- Visit a zoo or aquarium. These places have shows and interactive exhibits that teach people the importance of wildlife. Visitors receive science education in a fun way.
- Join a wildlife organization. Each one has a different mission. But they all teach ways to help conserve animals. Most have ways to "adopt" an endangered animal for a small fee.
- Plant a butterfly or pollinator garden. Once it is growing, keep track of how many pollinators are visiting.
- Keep cats indoors. Outdoor cats kill wild birds. And most don't even eat what they kill.

- Don't litter, of course. But go one step further. Pick up cans, bottles, and trash others have left behind. Animals can get injured by roadside trash or trapped inside it.

- Don't feed any animals except birds. Wildlife such as squirrels and deer will begin to rely on meals from humans. They will lose their natural fear. Other people might harm them.

Glossary

alliance
A group of people who are joined together in a project or cause.

conservation
The protection of animals, plants, and natural resources.

culverts
Drains or large pipes that allow water or animals to pass under a road or railroad.

economic
Relating to the way goods and services are made, sold, and bought.

ecosystem
Everything in a particular environment, from plants and animals to water and rocks.

nomadic
Moving from place to place instead of staying in one place.

poacher
Someone who catches or kills an animal illegally.

revive
To make something active or healthy again.

sanctuary
A place where people or animals are protected and given shelter.

sedated
Having been given drugs that cause sleep.

slaughterhouse
A place where animals are killed for their meat.

switch point
A movable rail that guides a train from one track to another.

Read More

Coey, Julia. *Animal Hospital: Rescuing Urban Wildlife*. Richmond Hill, ON: Firefly Books, 2015.

Hoare, Ben. *Eyewitness Endangered Animals.* DK Eyewitness. New York: DK Publishing, 2010.

Meeker, Clare Hodgson. *Rhino Rescue!: And More True Stories of Saving Animals.* Washington, DC: National Geographic Kids, 2016.

Newman, Aline Alexander. *Lucky Leopards!: And More True Stories of Amazing Animal Rescues.* Washington, DC: National Geographic Kids, 2014.

Index

About the Author

Patricia Hutchison is a former teacher. She has written dozens of nonfiction children's books about science, nature, history, and geography. She lives in South Carolina with her husband. They love to travel throughout the United States and to other countries.